Original title:
Grapes in the Vineyard

Copyright © 2025 Creative Arts Management OÜ
All rights reserved.

Author: George Mercer
ISBN HARDBACK: 978-1-80586-438-7
ISBN PAPERBACK: 978-1-80586-910-8

Poured Elegance

In a bottle, a dance goes on,
The wine whispers secrets till dawn.
Cork popped like a party balloon,
Giggling glasses join in the tune.

With a swirl and a sip we cheer,
Each drop brings laughter, never fear.
A splash of red on the tablecloth,
Oops! Looks like it's now a froth!

Chasing the Sun

Sun be shining, let's all play,
Find a grape to brighten the day.
We'll race the light, like silly fools,
A chase that breaks all the old rules.

With laughter echoing off the vines,
We toast our friendship and all the signs.
A picnic spread with snacks galore,
Whisper to the sun, 'We want more!'

Blossoms on the Breeze

Flowers giggle, sway in the air,
A bee provides tunes, without a care.
Dancing petals, oh what a sight,
Even the weeds know how to invite.

A breeze stirs up mischief and fun,
Chasing shadows on a lazy run.
Laughter is a sweet, fragrant wine,
To all the good times, we raise a line!

The Vineyard's Heartbeat

In the heart of the rows, a pulse is found,
Rhythm of laughter, all around.
The vines know how to harness a cheer,
With every stomp, there's nothing to fear.

Footloose and fancy, we twirl and spin,
Each little grape knows how to grin.
A harvest of jokes, so ripe and sweet,
Come join the party, lift your seat!

The Dance of the Foliage

In the garden, leaves take flight,
They shimmy and sway, what a sight!
Mice in tuxedos, they join the band,
Twirling and spinning, oh, isn't it grand?

Sunshine tickles the vines with glee,
Bumblebees buzzing a melody.
A squirrel shows off his latest move,
While the tomatoes are trying to groove!

The pumpkins chuckle, they know the score,
As the cucumbers roll, wanting more.
The figs are laughing, they bask in cheer,
While the radishes hide, oh dear, oh dear!

In this whimsical dance, all play their part,
Nature's shindig, a masterpiece of art.
So let us join in, don't be shy,
For the party's just starting, oh my, oh my!

Glistening Horizons

Under golden rays, a feast unfolds,
Brilliant colors that never grow old.
The walnuts gossip, they spill some tea,
While the carrots chuckle, 'It's wild, can't you see?'

Crows wearing hats, strut on the ground,
The laughter of nature is all around.
Each fruit and nut wears a smile so bright,
As they dance to the rhythm of day and night.

Ladybugs giggle, they play hide and seek,
While the shy little onions speak not a squeak.
What's this? A dance-off? Oh, what a blast!
The art of the harvest, coming in fast!

So come take a look, don your best shoes,
Join in this revelry, you cannot lose!
With friends all around and laughter that sings,
Together we'll celebrate all of these things!

Shadows Beneath the Canopy

When the sun shines bright, we all dance,
In shades of green, we take a chance.
The grapevine wriggles, they twist and twine,
Bouncing with giggles, oh, what a line!

Bumbling bees buzz, wearing little hats,
Join us in laughter, silly acrobats.
With leaves as our umbrellas, we play and sway,
In this grape-filled circus, all's fun and play!

The Sweetness of Abundance

Wobbling baskets, full to the brim,
What's in this harvest? A berry whim!
A feast for the senses, a feast for the soul,
With juice on our chins, we're on a roll!

Juggling fruit while wearing a grin,
Trying to catch them is where we begin.
Mirth in each squish, and laughter in mess,
Wine-stained shirts? Well, it's just our finesse!

Threads of Velvety Twilight

Under the twilight, we gather around,
With stories and giggles, no frown to be found.
The scent of the evening, so sweet and inviting,
We toast to the fun, and the night's just igniting.

As fireflies dance, our laughter flies high,
One grape to share? Oh, just give it a try!
With each tiny pop, there's a burst of delight,
We feast on this joy until the day turns to night!

Sipping from Nature's Cup

With cups held high, we sip in delight,
Nature's own brew, oh, what a sight!
Bubbles are giggling, floating up with cheer,
We savor the moment, while jokes fill the air.

One clumsy sip leads to whimsical spills,
Rolling down hills, oh, what silly thrills!
In this frothy chaos, we raise our cheer,
Each drop a treasure, my friends, gather near!

Secrets Beneath the Leaves

Beneath the green, a whisper flows,
A squirrel's stash, no one knows.
Plump treasures tucked with cheeky grins,
Even the rabbits join in the sins.

With tiny feet and twitchy tails,
They tickle the ground as they tell their tales.
As sunbeams dance on hidden loot,
Nature's playground becomes quite the hoot.

Laughter in the Tasting Room

In the tasting room, a riot ensues,
Wine floods the floor, mixed with blue shoes.
A sommelier makes a clumsy pour,
While guests giggle, wanting more.

Cheers erupt like fizz on the tongue,
'Will this one make us feel quite young?'
With laughter filling each glass and grin,
Who knew sipping could make us spin?

Embracing the Terroir

In soil rich with stories old,
Earthworms vie for a slice of gold.
The farmer laughs with a hand on his knee,
'Best crop yet, or is it just me?'

Sunsets blush like a drunken tease,
While raccoons toast with branches of trees.
A celebration for all things alive,
Where clumsy roots jive and thrive.

Sunkissed Serenity

Beneath bright skies where shadows play,
A dog rolls past in a delightful sway.
With tails a-wagging, they scatter and bark,
While picnic strawberries bloom in the park.

Sunkissed smiles glow on sunburned cheeks,
As bees attempt to invade with squeaks.
The warmth of the day, like a playful fling,
Who knew that simple joy could sing?

Echoes of Aged Oak

In the shade where shadows play,
The squirrels dance, come what may.
Old oak grumbles, won't let go,
Until the sun sets, then he'll glow.

They whispered secrets, tales they spun,
Of drunken bees and lazy fun.
On wooden benches, laughter spills,
Chasing dreams with joy that thrills.

Secrets of the Fruitful Grove

The snickering peaches hide in leaves,
Telling jokes like cheeky thieves.
Citrus smiles in morning light,
While the pears argue, ready to fight.

Cherries giggle as they dangle low,
Teasing the kids who stomp below.
In this grove of playful cheer,
Nature's humor rings crystal clear.

Raindrops and Richness

A raindrop fell with a playful splat,
Frogs jumped up; now that's a chat!
With splashes high, they laugh and croak,
As puddles form like nature's cloak.

Dewdrops giggle on leaves' soft skin,
As fluttering wings begin to spin.
Nature's wet dance, a joyful sight,
Making each moment feel just right.

Layers of Flavor and Time

With every layer, the crusty bread,
Whispers of moments, laughter spread.
Butter drips, the jam does tease,
A feast of fun, oh what a breeze!

Fruits of fun on the table lie,
Tarts and pies that make us sigh.
Among the flavors we often find,
A pinch of laughter, sweet and kind.

The Secret of Fermentation

In barrels tight, the juice can dance,
With giggles, bubbles, take a chance.
The yeast wears hats, oh what a sight,
As they party hard deep into the night.

With funky scents and wild, sweet flair,
They claim the secret recipe's rare.
But really, it's just a bit of fun,
And fermenting wisdom for everyone!

Between Row and Row

In the rows, the critters plot,
They steal the snacks, they're quite the lot.
A squirrel with charm, a raccoon with sass,
Remind me to check on the wine stash, alas!

The vines all whisper, 'Hey, did you know?',
The best grape jokes are best kept low.
So here's a riddle from the green parade,
What's a grape's favorite dance? The wine charade!

Nectar's Journey

A bee in a bowtie flies so neat,
Collecting the nectar, oh what a feat!
He zips through flowers, then takes a bow,
"I'm here for the party, just watch me now!"

The petals giggle in bright sunshine,
Pollen's the prize, oh how divine!
From bud to buzz, their laughter flows,
Do you think they dream of grapes in rows?

Under the Arbor's Gaze

Beneath the leaves, the shadows play,
Where critters meet for a sunny soirée.
"I brought the cheese!" chirps a wise old crow,
While ants parade with a fruit buffet show.

The sun dips low as the laughter grows,
Jokes about tannins, who knows how it goes?
With glasses clinking and smiles a-bright,
The merriment swells under starlit night!

Enchanted by Nature's Bounty

In fields where the sun laughs out loud,
The vines wear their greens like a proud shroud.
Bunches dangle, ripe without a care,
I swear they gossip about the fresh air.

The squirrels dance, they think they're the king,
While birds chirp joy, oh what songs they sing!
Nature's sweet bounty, a feast for the eye,
Every ripe cluster a reason to try.

Journeys of the Palate

Off we go on a munching spree,
With tasters and sippers as happy as can be.
Each plump treasure bursts with flavor and zest,
Like a party in my mouth, it's simply the best.

They roll and they tumble, these treats divine,
Turned into juice, oh how they shine!
With hiccups of joy, we lift our glass high,
To all those who laughed while they passed by.

The Taste of Cask and Barrel

Oh, what a tale does each barrel tell,
Stirring up laughter like a jolly old spell.
A sip here, a sip there, our faces aglow,
'Till we just can't tell the cork from the flow!

Barrels wobble, and laughter gets loud,
Would they prefer a drink or a crowd?
With each little toast, a mishap we share,
One little slip, and we're all in midair!

Vineyards in Bloom

Amidst the green, little critters play,
They frolic and tumble, as if on display.
Flowers burst forth, with chatter so spry,
While bees do the cha-cha, oh my, oh my!

Beneath the sun's wink, the day's pure delight,
We chase butterflies till the fall of night.
With baskets in hand, we giggle and cheer,
For nature's grand joke, let's all raise a beer!

Echoes in the Grape Arbor

In the shade, we laugh and cheer,
With cups raised high, we have no fear.
The vines laugh back, or so they seem,
As we dance around, in a tipsy dream.

A bird perched high, with a curious eye,
Mimics our jokes, oh my, oh my!
A squirrel joins in with a cheeky grin,
Stealing our snacks, let the fun begin!

A Palette of Purple

Brush strokes of fun, what a bright affair,
With squished toes, we paint without a care.
Purple splatters, laughter does bloom,
As we slip and slide in our grape-scented room.

The artist's cape, a flowing sight,
Draped on my friend, oh what a fright!
With laughter so loud, we can't stand still,
Our masterpiece made, with a dash and a spill.

Moonlit Late Harvest

Under the moon, we gather near,
With giggles that echo, nothing to fear.
The shadows dance in the soft night air,
As we play tag with moonbeams, unaware.

A rogue raccoon joins, his mask in place,
Sneaky and sly, he's quick in the chase.
With a clatter and crash, he snatches a bite,
We howl with laughter, what a silly sight!

The Serpent's Secret

In the twilight, whispers fly,
A serpent slithers, oh my, oh my!
With secrets tucked in his warm, green scales,
He chuckles and grins, as laughter prevails.

He tells us tales of the mess he's made,
Of grape-stomping parties, and sun's grand parade.
With a flick of his tongue, he winks at me,
"Join in the fun, there's plenty you'll see!"

Lush Bunches Under the Sun

In a patch where the sun does gleam,
Little fruits all dance and dream.
With laughter sweet and colors bright,
They tickle bees in pure delight.

One plump fellow starts to sway,
"I'm the star of the buffet!"
His friends all giggle, tipsy too,
"Hold your juice! We'll party true!"

Beneath the Green Canopy

Under leaves where whispers play,
Cheeky clusters hide away.
A squirrel peeks with eyes so wide,
"Looks like we're on a joyride!"

Beneath the shade, a chat begins,
"They'll never find us, let's win!"
A breeze comes by, with gentle cheer,
"Oh no! It's grape-ocalypse here!"

When the Wine Flows

As the sun dips, here they blend,
With a wink, they twist and bend.
"Let's raise a toast, we've come so far!"
They bubble up like a rising star.

The bottles cheer, "We'll dance tonight!"
"Fill us up, we'll feel just right!"
In each pour, a giggling spree,
"More fizzy fun, oh can't you see?"

Clusters of Twilight

As dusk embraces, shadows play,
Laughter in clusters leads the way.
One cheeky sprout calls for a dance,
"Join the grape-formance, take a chance!"

Twirling lightly, swaying wide,
"We're the grapes that never hide!"
With every twist, a joke is spun,
"Life's a party—join the fun!"

Sipping Sunsets

As twilight spills a golden hue,
The goblet jiggles, as I do.
I swig the laughter, mix a cheer,
Not sure if it's the drink or beer.

The juicy squish, a dance of taste,
In every sip, no drop to waste.
We toast to vines and silly clowns,
And tumble down in grassy gowns.

The mood is bright, the jokes are stale,
We giggle hard, set sail with ale.
The sun dips low, a happy blend,
In this fine hour, all rules we bend.

With shadows long, and voices loud,
Together we form a merry crowd.
Each sunset's sip, a tale retold,
In our silly hearts, pure joy unfolds.

The Language of the Leaves

Whispers swirl in rustling hues,
The leaves converse, with playful cues.
They gossip secrets, share a laugh,
In nature's theater, nature's path.

A squirrel prances, full of glee,
Stealing a charm from the wise old tree.
With every rustle, the laughter flies,
A symphony beneath the skies.

The foliage tells of summer scenes,
Of frolic, mischief, and lazy dreams.
Nature's chuckle fills the air,
As wild imaginations flare.

So when you wander, listen close,
To nature's quirks, the magic dose.
For every leaf unlocks the night,
In giggles found, pure delight.

Seasons of Abundance

In autumn's clutch, the bounty sprawls,
With laughter bright, as nature calls.
A pumpkin here and cider there,
We dance about without a care.

The harvest moon hangs overhead,
While we feast, with faces red.
Each morsel shared, a funny tale,
Of runaway carts and misfit pails.

Spring's antics bring a lively show,
With flowers sprouting high and low.
Honeybees buzz in a merry way,
As nature's jesters seize the day.

The summer sun, a wild friend,
Makes picnics last and never end.
We fill our cups, both light and free,
In every sip, absurdity.

Terracotta Paths and Wines

On winding lanes of crimson clay,
Our merry feet skip, twist, and sway.
With every step, a giggle reigns,
In terracotta dreams, our joy remains.

The barrels laugh, with voices bold,
Sharing stories, some untold.
Top hats made of corks, we wear,
As we prance about without a care.

In sunlight's gaze, we sip and grin,
With each small sip, the chaos begins.
Our clinking glasses, a rhythmic beat,
As our dance unfolds in jubilant heat.

Union of flavors, a chaotic whirl,
As mischief dances and laughter twirls.
In our whimsical world, all's well defined,
Terracotta paths and wines combined.

Bountiful Earth

In a field of luscious spills,
The round ones bounce like happy pills.
They giggle as they drink the sun,
A party unseen, oh what fun!

A farmer jigs with joy so spry,
As he checks the harvest, oh my!
Each cluster sways, a dance divine,
Nature's nectar, just don't whine!

Divine Elixir

A sip of joy in every glass,
With frothy hats that cheekily pass.
The toast is loud, the laughter bright,
That the night may lead to playful flight.

No need for worries, just joyful sips,
Each drop a wink, on silly trips.
In each swirl, a tale is found,
Of mishaps where the giggles abound!

The Serendipity of Fermentation

In a barrel hidden away,
Bubbles whisper, 'Come and play!'
They twist and turn, in friendly glee,
Turning sour into jubilee.

When the bubbles do their dance,
Laughter's sure to take a chance.
A hiccup here, a snort over there,
A fizzy trip without a care!

A Flavorful Journey

Each sip's a joyful, fruity ride,
With characters that bump and slide.
A splash of sparkle, a hint of zest,
A fragrant journey, quite the fest!

With every pour, a story flows,
Of funny things, like tiny toes.
The mouth giggles at the taste,
As memories swirl, nothing's waste!

En Route to the Decanter

In a bottle, dreams do swirl,
As cork pops off, it makes a twirl.
The path is set, a clink, a cheer,
To share the joy, let's make it clear!

With each step taken, laughter spills,
We race to pour, it surely thrills.
A splash on shirts, a clumsy feat,
The joy is full, can't be discreet!

A Symphony of Juices

In the field where laughter grows,
The fruits do jig with wiggly toes.
A dance of flavors, all in cheer,
Who knew that squishing meant such beer?

The sun shines bright, a hallelujah,
While pickers hum like a sweet tuba.
They stomp and hop, with sticky feet,
Creating wine that's hard to beat.

With every sip, the giggles flow,
Why must this barrel be so slow?
A toast to all the silly fun,
Let's drink to grapes, they've surely won!

So raise your glass, don't spill a drop,
Let's swirl and twirl, we just can't stop.
This symphony of joy is clear,
Cheers to the juice, let's live in cheer!

From Soil to Sip

Digging deep where worms do play,
Plants grow up to steal the day.
With roots so strong, and leaves so green,
Who knew dirt could taste so keen?

The harvest comes, it's time to cheer,
Workers sing and sip their beer.
In every bottle, tales unfold,
Of muddy shoes and stories bold.

The journey's long, yet oh so sweet,
From muck to munch, can't feel our feet.
A straw hat tipped quite askew,
Gives charm to every fermenting brew.

So slosh it round, then take a sip,
It's liquid laughter on your lip.
From soil to glass, oh what a trip!
Never thought I'd dance with a grape's flip!

The Color of Autumn's Kiss

Leaves are swirling like a twirl,
While grapes blush red, they twist and whirl.
Mother Nature's cheeky tease,
Beneath the trees, we're lost at ease.

Pies are baking, cider flows,
In the air, a breezy prose.
A color dance of yellow and gold,
Nothing says "fun" quite like bold.

We stomp and dance, the juicy way,
Making friends with every spray.
With laughter warm like a sunlit haze,
We'll toast to autumn and all its ways.

So swirl that cup, let joy unmask,
The colors bright, we cheer and bask.
In playful tones, we sip and giggle,
As autumn whispers, let's dance and wiggle!

Pouring Passion into Glass

A clay pot's wink, a flirty pour,
With every splash, we all want more.
The bottle smiles, it's feeling grand,
Sloshing joy in every hand.

Corks pop loud, it's quite the scene,
As laughter bubbles, joy's routine.
Each drop a giggle, each sip a smile,
It's serious fun, let's stay a while.

Let's paint the night with shades of cheer,
Every swig brings buddies near.
With friends around, the moments fly,
Passion clinks under the sky.

So lift your glass, let spirits soar,
In every sip, there's room for more.
Pouring laughter, swirling glass,
With every taste, good times will last!

Moonlight on the Bunches

Under a moon that glows so bright,
Bunches giggle, what a sight!
They whisper tales of silly dreams,
Dancing under silver beams.

The grapes have jokes, oh what a tease,
They share puns with the buzzing breeze.
Rolling down like a playful ball,
Who knew fruit could have a ball?

Some wear hats, a silly crown,
Others joke, don't let us down!
With laughter wrapped in dewy skin,
Every night's a fruity win!

So toast with laughter, join the cheer,
In this orchard, fun is near!
Sipping sweets, with friends so dear,
Together here, we have no fear.

Recycling the Past

In the cellar where secrets lay,
Old bottles giggle and sway.
Whispers of the fervent past,
They pop the corks and have a blast.

Once a vintage, now a tale,
Moldy memories, a funny trail.
"Remember when we spilled that red?"
All the corks nod, no one's dead!

The labels scrunch up, bear a grin,
As they recall the fun within.
Each sip a moment, they say so wise,
They age like jokes, oh what a prize!

So raise your glass, don't hold back,
Recycling laughs, leave no track!
In this cellar, time stands still,
With winks and giggles, it's such a thrill.

Woven in the Soil

Deep in the earth, where the roots reside,
A comedy of sprouts, with nothing to hide.
They tell stories of who tripped last,
While tangled together, they question the past.

"I swear I saw a worm in a hat!"
Cried one young sprout, then they all sat.
"Did it dance? Or just wiggle away?"
The laughter echoes, brightening the day.

As the sun shines down, they take a stance,
"Let's grow tall and show our dance!"
With a shimmy and shake, their leaves unfurl,
Nature's jesters, spinning in twirls.

So join this show, beneath the green,
In the soil where laughter's seen.
With roots so deep and hearts so free,
Life's a giggle, come laugh with me!

The Poetry of the Palate

A splash of color, a taste so fine,
Each nibble's a joke, oh how they shine!
From tangy to sweet, a playful blend,
In the realm of taste, there's never an end.

"Is that a berry or a cheeky grape?"
They tease each other, trying their shape.
With flavors bold, and scents that play,
They paint the tongue in a funny way.

A sip of red winks and laughs,
It swirls in glasses, unleashing its gaffs.
"Oh, that's too sour for my sweet tooth!"
They giggle and joke, sharing the truth.

So savor each bite, let laughter flow,
In taste's great comedy, join the show!
With every course, a chuckling cheer,
The poetry of flavor, let's all adhere!

Revelry of the Lush Canes

In the green, the bunches sway,
With tiny critters taking play.
They bounce and touch, so full of cheer,
Who knew a vine could have such beer?

A sneaky bird, with a beak so bright,
Plays peek-a-boo, what a funny sight!
The canes do jig, they twist and shout,
Their leafy dance leaves no doubt!

Sun and Soil's Embrace

Under sunbeams, they form a gang,
Roots dance below, while branches sang.
The soil whispers, oh so bold,
"Let's make this tale of wine unfold!"

The sun grins wide, a golden boost,
While worms below, throw parties, goosed!
Earthy laughter fills the air,
As tiny bugs join in the flair.

Harvest Dreams

The baskets wait for treasures bright,
While squirrels scheme their daring flight.
The fruit's so round, they play tough hide,
Pretending they're shy, but oh, they bide!

With laughter loud from every vine,
The pickers joke, "This one's divine!"
A friendly race, to fill their pail,
As giggles fly on wavy trail.

The Whispering Vines

In the breeze, the tender talks,
Of sneaky snails who stroll like clocks.
They swap their tales of sunlit glee,
Creating mischief by the spree!

A raccoon peers from leafy shade,
Countless naps in the sun have made.
"Oh, what joy, in this green cocoon,
Who knew dirt could host such a tune?"

Sweetness on the Breeze

A cluster sways with glee,
Whispering jokes to the bee.
"Why do we hang on a vine?"
"Because we're too sweet to be wine!"

Bunches laugh in the sun,
Creating mischief and fun.
"Watch out for the old vine's pranks!"
"They'll surely take us to the banks!"

The breeze carries giggles around,
As juicy puns tumble down.
"On a salad, we're quite the tease!"
"Dressed up in laughter and cheese!"

A plump one winks at the sun,
"Life's a picnic, let's run!"
Beneath the bubbly grape leaves,
A party where no one grieves!

Shadows of the Old Trellis

Old trellis stands tall and proud,
Casting humor on the crowd.
"What do you call a grape that's shy?"
"A vine that wants to say hi!"

Laughter lingers in the shade,
Cool and crisp, and freshly made.
"How do grapes keep their color?"
"With a tan that's never duller!"

Beneath the vines, shadows dance,
Twisting in a funny prance.
"Why did the grape cross the path?"
"To escape the old vine's wrath!"

The whispers of fruit echo near,
Tickling the leaves without fear.
Old trellis sways, it knows the deal,
In laughter we find our appeal!

Liquid Gold in the Glass

Golden liquid, shining bright,
Jokes swirl round in morning light.
"Why don't we ever play cards here?"
"Because the jokes are too unclear!"

Sipping joy, we tip our hats,
To cheeky jokes and playful chats.
"What do you call a bottle with pride?"
"A vintage that won't hide!"

The taste tickles, a laughing spree,
With every sip, we feel so free.
"Did you hear the one 'bout the cork?"
"It popped out to go for a walk!"

Swirling flavors in each pour,
Tasting laughter, there's always more.
With each clink, our spirits soar,
Liquid gold we can't ignore!

An Ode to the Old Vines

Old vines wobbly yet wise,
Sprouting tales beneath the skies.
"What's a vine's favorite dance?"
"The twist and shout, given a chance!"

They've seen seasons come and go,
With stories that ebb and flow.
"Why do vines never get stressed?"
"They know how to unwind and jest!"

Wrapped in laughter, roots run deep,
While silly secrets they keep.
"Have you met the shy little sprout?"
"He's just too 'vine' to come out!"

In their presence, we can't help but grin,
These old souls remind us to win.
With humor growing where they twine,
Here's to life, and the old vines!

Moonlit Trails of Temptation

In the glow of night, so bright,
A little critter steals a bite.
He dances round with such delight,
"Who knew these fruits could cause a fight?"

With every munch, the laughter grows,
As sticky fingers steal the shows.
The moonlight beams, it surely knows,
A party starts when jammy toes!

A raccoon's plan, so sly, so slick,
He dodges traps with crafty tricks.
The fruit is ripe, it's rather thick,
And all the neighbors yell, "He's quick!"

They laugh and cheer, the night's still young,
While toasting tales with songs unsung.
In rows they run, and oh, how fun,
Who knew that mischief had begun?

Where Sweetness Meets the Sun

In fields so bright, the bees do hum,
The flowers blush, oh what's to come?
With every drop of honeyed fun,
They scheme and plot, just like a pun!

Sipping nectar in the rays,
The sunlit game, a sweetened craze.
The bumblebees dance in a haze,
"Let's have a ball," their buzzing says!

The butterflies join in the rush,
A colorful, chaotic crush.
With every sip, there's quite the hush,
"Did someone say—let's feel the flush?"

As laughter lifts, the day's complete,
With fruity bites, we can't be beat.
Together we'll share this grand sweet treat,
And dance until we're all on our feet!

A Harvest Moon's Embrace

Under moonlight, farmers cheer,
Their baskets full, they've nipped some beer.
With every sip, their worries clear,
And laughter echoes from ear to ear.

The pumpkin smiles, the squash does roll,
With every drink, we've lost control.
"Let's juggle fruits! Come on, be bold!"
The scene is set, a merry stroll.

An old goat laughs, he steals the show,
Grazing grapes as if he knows.
With all this fun, where does it go?
"Let's make some jam!" they yell, "Oh no!"

As moonbeams shine on this delight,
The harvest sings through the night.
With juggling acts and silly fright,
The fest concludes, what pure delight!

Whispers of the Old Roots

Beneath the vines, the chatter spreads,
As critters plot with little threads.
They tango 'round with grape-like heads,
And tell the tales of sleepy beds.

With every twist, the gopher grins,
"Let's play a game, I'll take some wins!"
While squirrels throw an acorn spin,
The laughter stirs where fun begins.

"Oh dear," the old owl starts to hoot,
"These mischievous fellows, what a brute!"
But even he joins in the loot,
As fruits pass by, they shake their boot!

So let us dance where roots entwine,
With all our troubles left behind.
For every laugh that we define,
Is worth a glass of that sweet wine!

A Dance of Sweetness

In the morning sun they sway,
Round and round, they laugh and play.
Sticky fingers, a burst of cheer,
Who let the chickens wander near?

With each stomp, they sing a tune,
A waltz beneath the bright full moon.
Footwear slips, oh what a sight,
Who knew squishing could feel so right?

A jolly romp, the barrels thump,
As cheerful beetles do the jump.
Casks do jiggle, laughter loud,
It's a stomping party, such a crowd!

At twilight's glow, they take a seat,
Dancing feet now sore but sweet.
Beneath the stars, they raise a cheer,
To all the joy that brings us here!

Sunlit Bounty

Under the sun, they bask and grin,
With cheeky smiles as the day begins.
A swarm of crew all wearing hats,
Swatting flies from plump, fat brats.

Laughter bounces, tossing bunches,
As little bugs make silly munches.
The baskets tip, oh what a mess,
Nature's jewels, we must confess!

A blooper reel of comical slips,
Fruits fly out like clumsy ships.
One lad trips, down goes his snack,
With sticky hands, he'll never look back!

As night unfurls its velvet cloak,
Up high they toast, let's raise a joke.
With cheeky grins and tales to share,
The golden hours, oh how we dare!

The Vineyard Murmurs

Whispers glide on the warm, soft breeze,
Where pixies plot beneath the trees.
They spill their secrets, giggles spread,
As squirrels rush off with crumbs of bread.

The jars of nectar, oh what a thrill,
Stirring oodles of giggly spills.
A raccoon dances with flair untamed,
With dizzy spins, he's proudly named!

Beneath arched canopies, shadows play,
Creating antics, oh what a day.
Polka dots on shirts, what a riot,
Garden games, a raucous diet!

As twilight whispers a gentle hum,
Jovial hearts beat like a drum.
With laughter ringing, the night draws near,
In echoes sweet, let's share a cheer!

Treading the Glistening Juice

The crew assembles, eager feet,
Prepared to squish and make the sweet.
With every stomp, the squelch they hear,
Like high school dances, full of cheer!

Flailing arms, oh what a sight,
A little hop, a wobbly flight.
One slips down, the frolic grows,
With sticky laughs, the chaos flows!

Barrels spinning, a merry mess,
In joyful glee, they must confess.
Faces glisten, playful splashes,
As feet get tangled in silly clashes!

As sun fades low, the fun won't stop,
With raucous cheers, they all say "plop!"
To bubbling bowls and jovial song,
In this wild game, we all belong!

Wine-Stained Memories

In the cellar's dusky glow,
A bottle slipped, oh what a show!
We laughed and danced, red stains on shoes,
Who knew the cork could so easily lose?

Friends gathered round the spilled delight,
With belly laughs that turned to slight.
The clumsy cheers and tipsy spree,
Each drop a tale, oh what a glee!

With every sip, the stories grew,
Of wild grapes that bravely flew.
We toasted to the night so fine,
In every glass, a memory divine!

So raise a cup to the stains we wear,
To silly times, and laughter rare.
For every slip brings joy anew,
In our wine-stained world, so bright and true!

Roots Embraced by Earth

Deep in the soil, where the critters creep,
Roots tickle each other, a secret to keep.
They giggle and twist, planning a prank,
To tickle the toes of the passing tank!

Worms throw a party, all dressed in brown,
While moles do a dance, spinning around.
The peasants above sip their vintage delight,
Unaware of the root-tango taking flight!

When rain hits the leaves, it's a splashing spree,
The vines shake their heads, saying, "Let's be free!"
They grow wild and strong, creating a scene,
While down below, they conspire unseen.

So next time you sip, just think of the play,
Of roots underfoot, in their whimsical way.
For every good drop starts down in the dirt,
With laughter and mischief, where magic does flirt!

A Symphony of Ripeness

In the orchard, a concert starts,
The apples join in, sharing their parts.
Banjos of berries join the fray,
While pears hum along, in their mellow way.

The cherries chirp high, with a wink in their hue,
"Dance, dance!" they cry, "We're ripe through and through!"
The plump purple fellows, they roll in delight,
All jamming together in the warm, golden light.

An audience of bees buzz in tune,
With fuzzy little jackets, under the moon.
They sway to the rhythm, nectar in hand,
In this fruity fest, every note's well planned!

So take a sip, let joy take flight,
From berries a'gather, a festive sight.
In each funky note, let tastes intertwine,
In this merry orchestra, we all wine and dine!

The Color of Harvest

As the sun dips low and shadows dance,
Fields turn to gold, what a classy romance!
The pumpkins parade in their orange pride,
While cabbages green bashfully hide.

The corn sends a message, tall and absurd,
"Hey, look at us, we're quite the herd!"
With whispers of butter, and sly little laughs,
They dream of their future in savory drafts.

Ripe tomatoes scatter, all round like stars,
Laughing so hard, they forget their jars.
The squash picks a fight, all bumpy and bold,
While berries gang up, their sweetness uncontrolled.

So celebrate colors, let laughter take lead,
For harvest is silly, and always a treat.
With each joyful bite, from root to the pea,
Let's toast to the fun in our earthy jubilee!

The Timeless Vine

Beneath the sun, they twist and twine,
The little fruits with faces fine.
They giggle loud, they sway and dance,
In this fine world, they take their chance.

Crawling critters, cheeky and spry,
Join the party, oh my oh my!
A snail in shades, a bug with flair,
Together they form a wild affair.

Clusters whisper funny tales,
Of drunken bees and wind that wails.
They chatter 'bout the grapes they'll be,
As ripe as dreams, oh wait and see!

With each twist of vines, there's a jest,
Nature's comedy, simply the best.
When harvest comes, they claim their throne,
In bottles marked "Please leave us alone!"

Nature's Alchemy

In a barrel, secrets brew,
Flavors mingle, a playful crew.
What will they pop out as today?
A circus, a dance, or a cabaret?

The sun and rain, they share a joke,
As bubbles rise and vapors poke.
The fruit gets wild, begins to sway,
Screaming, "Pour me, let's start the play!"

The cork pops off with lots of cheer,
Spilling laughter, spreading good cheer.
'We're all a bit tipsy,' they proclaim,
'Join us, friend, let's play this game!'

In every sip, a giggle's found,
Of nature's fun, it's glorious sound.
The magic works, it's plain to see,
Jesting with joy, oh let it be!

Memories in Each Sip

Each bottle tells a tale so fine,
Of days spent lost among the vine.
A squirrel that danced, a sparrow that sang,
The joy of nature, a sweet boomerang.

With every pour, a story flows,
Of secret picnics and silly foes.
Laughter bubbles, a wobbly ride,
As memories cheer and swell with pride.

Here's to the days of whimsy and cheer,
To fruit that giggles, to joy held dear.
In every taste, a funny delight,
A toast to the sun setting bright.

So lift your glass and take a sip,
Let's toast to the vines and let laughter rip!
Each sip's a hug from the past,
Full of giggles, meant to last!

The Chorus of the Harvesters

A motley crew with baskets wide,
They jig and jive, they take in stride.
Their songs of work, funny and bold,
Their voices sweet, their tales retold.

With every cut, a joke is made,
"Did you hear about the wine parade?"
Each fruit a gem, they grin and sing,
Humming to the joy that harvest brings.

One joker slips, a tumble and roll,
The others gasp and lose control!
"How many pickers does it take?" they cry,
"To make a splash? Just you and I!"

So they laugh as they gather round,
In nature's dance, their joy is found.
A raucous bunch, they're never tame,
Harvesting fun is their claim to fame!

Pressing Time

In the cellar, a clamor and cheer,
A squishy stomp brings laughter near.
Bottles uncorked, the corks fly fast,
"Watch your heads! It's quite the blast!"

With every step, a squelchy sound,
The fruit takes flight, round and round.
Squeezed and squashed, what a sight,
As jugs overflow, what pure delight!

The more we stomp, the more we spill,
This juice is potent; it gives a thrill.
All revel here in fruity jest,
Who knew that pressing could be the best?

So let's raise our cups, toast the fun,
To sweet, sticky mischief, more to come!
With laughter and fruit, we toast divine,
It's pressing time—come sip and dine!

Autumn's Embrace

Leaves twirl down, a graceful dance,
While fuzzy friends take a tipsy chance.
Ripe morsels hang, so plump and round,
Squirrels gather, the feast they've found.

Sunshine dips with golden flair,
The harvest steals the evening air.
Bees buzz by—what a lively crowd!
It's a party that's just a bit too loud!

Chubby raccoons in a wine-soaked spree,
Wobbling 'round, who needs to be free?
Under the moon, the giggles grow,
As critters join in the autumn glow.

So let's toast to this messy fun,
In the crisp air where laughter's spun!
With every sip and every cheer,
Autumn's embrace draws silly near!

A Tapestry of Tales

Gather 'round, for stories unfold,
Of mischief and laughter, the bravest bold.
With every pour, a tale sets sail,
Of runaway carts and a grape-sized whale!

One feller tripped on the vine in haste,
His friends all laughed as he fell with grace.
A twist of fate, a tangle of fun,
Stories born from a race well-run.

A wise old frog croaks out advice,
"Don't hurry through, take your time, be nice!"
With toast and giggles, they share and sip,
Each glass a laugh, every tale a quip.

A tapestry we weave, with jokes and glee,
In this rambunctious, fruity jubilee.
Raise a glass and toast to the night,
For life's little mishaps are pure delight!

Late Afternoon Glow

The sun hangs low, a golden tease,
As bees buzz by with chilling ease.
Baskets piled high, the spoils divine,
Chortles and snickers merge with the wine.

Pies on the window, oh, what a sight!
'Trick or treat,' they chirp with delight.
A raccoon prances, gives a grand show,
In late afternoon's warm, silly glow.

Bottle caps pop, time to unwind,
Giggling daisies dance in the wind.
While feet tap tunes to the fruity refrain,
What a delight, this whimsical gain!

So savor the laughter, let worries flee,
For late afternoons bring pure jubilee.
With every sip, let cheerfulness flow,
In this mirthful moment, let joy overflow!

Harvest of Sunlit Spheres

In rows so neat, they hang with grace,
Chubby little orbs, a merry face.
They giggle and dance in the warm sun's blaze,
Waiting to join in the evening's praise.

A plump one spills juice, making a mess,
A sticky situation, oh what a bless!
They laugh at the crush, saying, 'What a ride!'
'Thank goodness we're sweet; we take it in stride!'

With glasses raised high, the cheer does not end,
As silly faces and laughter blend.
The silly jokes flow, like the drink in the cup,
With every great sip, we all lift it up!

So gather 'round friends, relish this treat,
From the spillage of wine to our dancing feet.
Let joy in the sun and the fun times abound,
In this harvest of laughter, together we're found.

The Wine's Whisper

A cozy chat spills from the bottle's mouth,
Whispers of summer, joy pouring south.
'Oh, how I love the toes in the dirt!'
In the cool of the shade, where we quench our hurt.

Little clusters plotting all night,
'Tomorrow we're bottled! We'll take flight!'
They snicker and tease as the corkscrew spins,
A hilarious fate for these cheeky twins.

With each little sip, come smiles all around,
The bottle begs laughter, us merry and sound.
'Let's swirl and let's slosh, pour me some more!'
Cheers to the harvest, let's dance on the floor!

In glasses we dare to spin tales so bright,
Of belly-laugh truths under stars each night.
A toast to the whispers, to jokes that amuse,
With full hearts and glasses, we happily cruise.

A Tapestry of Vines

Woven through hills, a green-clad delight,
Each twist and each turn, a comical sight.
They tangle and titter, sharing old tales,
Of mishaps and folly in sun-drenched trails.

The bugs buzz off, thinking they're big,
While the leaves giggle, doing a jig.
'We're the curtain for sunshine's play,
Stealing the show in our leafy ballet!'

From harvest to crush, a festival spins,
With snorting and snickering, oh, where to begin?
The juice spills like secrets, under a smile,
As we dance with the humor, let's stay for a while.

So join in the fun, let's frolic and scheme,
For this tapestry here weaves joy in a dream.
With laughter as sweet as the nectar we find,
Let mischief unfurl, and all hearts be kind!

Nectar of the Earth

Down in the valley where good times grow,
Silly little fruits put on quite a show.
They chuckle and wink, 'We're sweet as can be,
Let's party on down with glee, just wait and see!'

A toast to the soil, the mud and the muck,
Where each juicy treasure has found its own luck.
They giggle and bounce, like they're part of the chase,
'Last one to the barrel has egg on their face!'

With frothy frolics and jokes so spry,
It spills from the cask, oh my, oh my!
Laughing reminds us of all we've been through,
As we sip from our glasses and dance 'round anew.

So raise your cup high and share in delight,
The nectar of laughter that makes the heart light.
As bottles tremble near, and stories unfold,
Let's laugh 'til tomorrow, both merry and bold!

Stories in Each Cluster

In a land of twists and turns, they stand,
Little orbs of laughter, oh so grand.
Whispers of secrets in every bite,
Drunk on their sweetness, oh what a sight!

Beneath the sun, they dance and sway,
A little too tipsy at the end of the day.
Their tales of summer, wild and bold,
With every pluck, new stories told!

The rumble of laughter rides the breeze,
As they wiggle and jiggle, the sassy tease.
"Oh, pick me first!" they try to shout,
Yet tumble and roll, that's what they're about!

Bottled up giggles, and hiccups of cheer,
Each cluster promises good times near.
So gather 'round for a playful feast,
Where joy is the harvest, and laughter, the yeast!

A Toast to the Gleaners

Raise your glass, oh merry crew,
To those who gather with a wild view!
With baskets rolling, laughter flows,
A funny sight, as everyone knows!

Beneath the sun, they bump and trip,
Their little dance, a silly slip.
"What's that you found? A treasure rare!"
"Oh no, it's just my messy hair!"

With tiny hands, they tumble bound,
Under the leaves, fun can be found.
They laugh and cry, with playful glee,
As juicy nuggets tumble free!

So here's a cheer, through every stem,
For those who revel in the vineyard's hem.
With every sip, may your heart grow fonder,
As we toast to joy, and let our hearts wander!

Harvest Moon and Twinkling Stars

When the moon casts shadows over the leaves,
The tiny orbs giggle, pulling their sleeves.
"Let's make a party, we'll dance all night!"
So under the stars, they start their flight!

With drunken sways and cheeky grins,
They're spinning in circles, oh where to begin?
"Who let the bugs in?" one gently bleats,
A party so wild, what a night of treats!

The path is a jigsaw of giggles and mess,
As they tumble and roll, causing a distress.
"Oh, wear your shoes!" comes a shrill little shout,
Yet barefooted they run, filled with joyful clout!

So under the harvest, join the spree,
With moonlit laughter, it's wild and free.
Cheers to the fun that the night uncovers,
With twinkling stars, let's toast to our lovers!

Ray of Gold

In a field where sunshine paints the ground,
Little spheres of joy dance all around.
They shout and cheer, not shy at all,
Under the sun, they frolic and sprawl!

Beneath the boughs, they play a game,
"Catch me if you can!" they laugh with fame.
A slip here, a spill, oh what a show,
As they tumble and roll, their colors glow!

With every burst, a chuckle's revealed,
Their juicy jokes perfectly concealed.
"Oh no, don't squish me!" one little cries,
As they giggle and bumble beneath the skies!

So here's to the rays of laughter bright,
That beam through the leaves, a joyful site.
Take a sip of joy, let's lighten the mood,
For life's a grand party, and friendship's the food!

www.ingramcontent.com/pod-product-compliance
Lightning Source LLC
Chambersburg PA
CBHW071126130526
44590CB00056B/2707